The Tudors

Paul Noble

GW00802006

Contents

Introduction

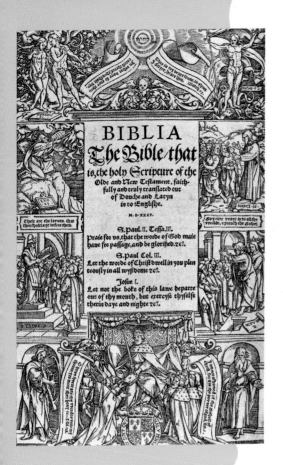

Everyone has heard of Queen Elizabeth, William Shakespeare and Sir Francis Drake. They have also seen pictures of **Tudor** men and women dressed in very colourful and elaborate clothes.

Not all the Tudors were famous or rich. Even so, many people believe that Tudor times were one of the most exciting and glamorous in our history. As you read about the Armada and the Field of Cloth of Gold as well as the lives of ordinary people living over 400 years ago, you will be able to judge for yourself.

◀ The first complete Bible in English was published in 1536.

Henry VII 1485 – 1509	Henry VIII 1509 – 1547

▶ Henry VIII lived at Hampton Court.

◄ Edward VI was nine when he became king and died of tuberculosis when he was sixteen.

► Mary I was a Catholic. In the five years of her reign she tried to make England Catholic too. Many **Protestants** were burnt at the stake.

 **Edward VI
1547 – 1553**

			Elizabeth I 1558 – 1603

 **Mary I
1553 – 1558**

► The Armada, sent by Spain to invade England in 1588.

Who were the Tudors?

The Tudor Age began in a field. In 1485, Henry Tudor's army fought against the army of Richard III near Market Bosworth in Leicestershire. At the end of the day's battle, Henry was victorious. He became Henry VII, the first Tudor **monarch.** The Tudor **dynasty** ruled for over a hundred years.

We have a good idea of what the kings and queens looked like from painted **portraits.** Most English people in Tudor times never met their king or queen, but they learned what they looked like from these portraits. Portraits could lie. Painters tried to improve the appearance of the people they painted in order to please them, so we have to compare portraits with other evidence.

Henry VIII

Henry VIII reigned for 38 years. As a young man he was handsome and athletic, but painters had to hide his fatness as he grew older. He desperately wanted a son, which is one reason why he married six times.

The **Ambassador** from Venice wrote this about Henry VIII,

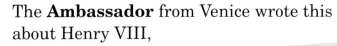

> He is a good musician; composes well; is a most talented horseman; a fine jouster; speaks good French, Latin and Spanish; is very religious and is very fond of hunting and tennis.

◀ Henry VIII aged 49. His shoulders have been painted large and his arm bent, to make him look strong and important.

Henry VIII's wives

While still married to his first wife, Henry VIII fell passionately in love with Anne Boleyn. He wrote numerous love letters to her.

...No more now for lack of time hoping quite soon to tell you by word of mouth the pangs I have suffered through your absence. Written by the hand of the secretary who wishes himself at this time with you privately, and who is and ever will be.

Your loyal and most assured servant.

(H seeks AB no other R)

▲ Part of a letter written by Henry VIII to Anne Boleyn.

▼ Anne Boleyn, mother of Elizabeth I.

When Henry finally married Anne, she gave birth to a daughter, Elizabeth. But Henry turned against Anne and his love became hate. She was accused of being unfaithful and was executed.

This is what happened to Henry's wives.

First wife	Catherine of Aragon (mother of Mary I)	Divorced
Second wife	Anne Boleyn (mother of Elizabeth I)	Beheaded
Third wife	Jane Seymour	Died after giving birth to a son (the future Edward VI)
Fourth wife	Anne of Cleves	Divorced
Fifth wife	Catherine Howard	Beheaded
Sixth wife	Catherine Parr	Outlived Henry

Anne Boleyn's daughter

Princess Elizabeth was born at Greenwich Palace, a quiet country house on the River Thames. She was a very intelligent child. When she was only six years old it was said that she was as wise as if she was forty. In those days, it was unusual to bother with educating a woman, but exceptions were made. Elizabeth became one of the most educated women of her time. By the age of 10 she knew Italian, French and Latin. She went on to learn Greek and Spanish.

Her teacher Roger Ascham wrote, "Her mind has no womanly weakness, her perseverance is equal to that of a man, and her memory long keeps what it quickly picks up." He praised her so highly he thought that he would not be believed. "I am inventing nothing, there is no need," he continued.

▶ Elizabeth, aged 16, a princess.

As Elizabeth grew up she was in constant danger from her enemies, especially those who thought that she might plot against Queen Mary. But Elizabeth was careful as well as clever and avoided execution. When Mary died she became queen.

Elizabeth became one of the most famous Tudor monarchs. Although Elizabeth lived longest (70 years) and reigned longest (44 years), she never married or had children, so she was the last Tudor. By using her skill and determination she kept England a peaceful country.

A German traveller said,

The Queen, in her sixty-fifth year of her age, is very majestic; her face oblong, fair but wrinkled; her eyes small, yet black and pleasant; her nose a little hooked; her lips narrow; and her teeth black (from too great a use of sugar); she had in her ears two pearls, with very rich drops; she wore false hair, and that red.

◀ Elizabeth, the Queen.

◗ **a** Which is most accurate: a written description or a painting of someone? How might you tell?

◪ **a** Study the painting of Elizabeth I on this page closely. Where is it wrong or distorted? (Think of the shape of the human body.) Can you explain why?

b Compare the two pictures of Elizabeth and say something about:
the way she is standing   clothes   jewellery
her character and expressions   hair style   make-up
objects in the picture   background and colours.

c Closely examine one of the portraits using a magnifying glass. Describe the clothes. Say what you think they are made of. You could make a collage picture matching the colours and materials.

△ **a** Using as much information as you can find, write a short life-story (**biography**) of a Tudor king or queen.

The Tudor Realm

There was no United Kingdom of Britain and Ireland in Tudor times. The Tudors ruled England and part of France. The last English city in France, Calais, was not recaptured by the French until 1558.

Scotland was a separate nation with its own monarch. The two countries were not good neighbours. England and Scotland fought many battles. The fiercest took place at Flodden in 1513. When the battle was over, the defeated Scots had lost their king, three bishops, eleven earls, fifteen lords and 10 000 soldiers.

Wales was joined to England by an Act of Union in 1536. In Wales people often spoke two languages, as they did in Cornwall. A foreign visitor described

▼ A map showing the Tudor realm.

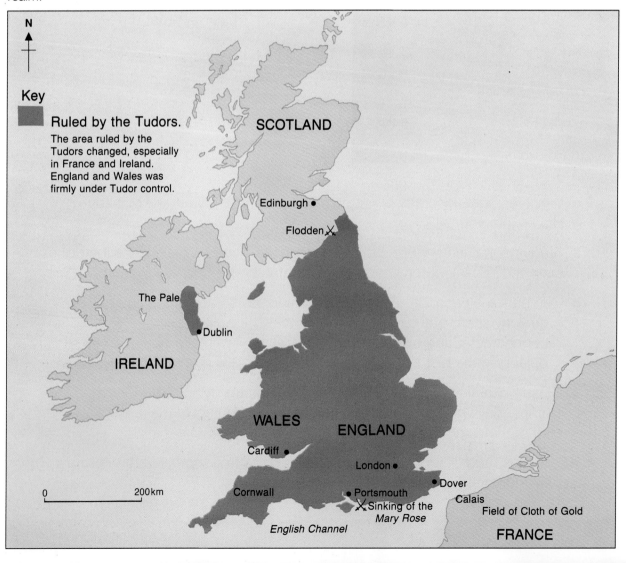

N

Key

Ruled by the Tudors.
The area ruled by the Tudors changed, especially in France and Ireland. England and Wales was firmly under Tudor control.

SCOTLAND

Edinburgh ●

Flodden ✕

The Pale

● Dublin

IRELAND

WALES

ENGLAND

Cardiff ●

London ●

● Dover

0   200km

Cornwall

● Portsmouth
✕ Sinking of the
   Mary Rose

Calais

Field of Cloth of Gold

English Channel

FRANCE

Tudor England as 'one land but three languages, English, Welsh and Cornish.' Lords and ladies, rich landowners and educated men, spoke English and called themselves English wherever they lived.

▲ Richly dressed gentlemen in procession at the Westminster Tournament, two years before the Battle of Flodden. Tournaments were war games where fighting skills were practised.

Most of Ireland was **Gaelic** and ruled by independent chiefs. Both Gaelic Irish and 'English' Irish lived in Ireland. The English mainly lived in a narrow strip near the eastern coast called The Pale. The Tudors tried to get the Gaelic Irish to learn English and to follow English customs. Henry VIII also decided to call himself 'King of Ireland'. Eventually there was a long, bloody and confused war.

◑ **a** If you were an important person in the Tudor government, which languages would it be most useful to speak. Why?

◪ **a** On an outline map of Britain mark all the places that have been mentioned so far. Draw labels that give a fact about each place.

  b Compare a modern map of the British Isles with the map here. List some of the main differences.

△ **a** Find out the names of some ruling dynasties that came before and after the Tudors.

Land and People

John Norden, a map maker, was instructed by Queen Elizabeth I to 'travel through England and Wales to make more perfect descriptions and charts.'

Travelling mainly on horse-back, he began a great survey of the Tudor realm just as the queen had commanded him. The notes and maps that he made give us some idea of what the land and the people were like.

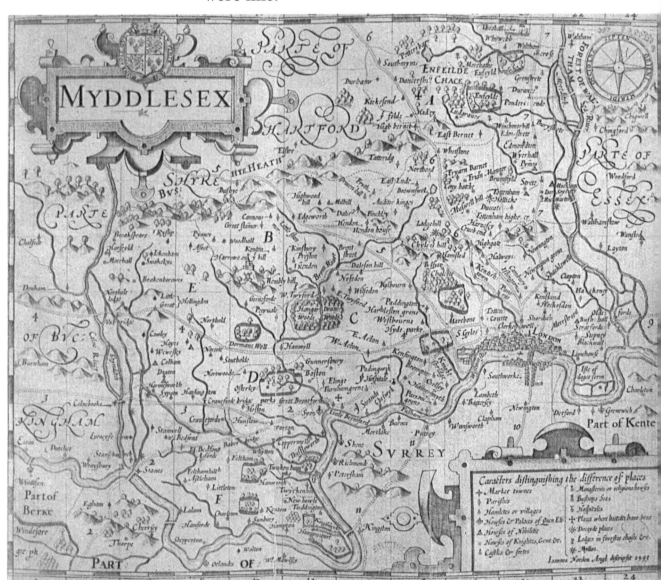

Can you find the City of London on John Norden's map?

Northumberland is chiefly noted for swift horses and sea coals, a rough country and hardly tilled, inhabited by fierce people.

Lancashire is plentiful of oats and great beeves.

Somerset is bad for winter travelling so wet and weely, so miry and moorish it is.

St Pancras is usually haunted by rogues, vagabonds and thieves. Walk not there too late.

Sussex is divided into downs full of sheep and woodland full of iron mines.

▲ Ploughing the fields.

▶ Looking after sheep.

London

Apart from London, towns were little more than large villages. London grew and grew. It had 50 000 people in 1520 and four times that many when Elizabeth I died. It was overcrowded, dirty and smelly. Londoners called one street, 'Stinking Lane,' because it smelt so much. Yet London could also be very rich and grand.

▲ The Tower of London and London bridge.

An Italian visitor wrote,

London is defended by handsome walls on the northern side. Within these stands a very strongly defended castle on the banks of the river. There are also other great buildings, especially a beautiful and convenient bridge over the Thames, of many marble arches, which has on it many shops built of stone and mansions and even a church of considerable size. Nowhere have I seen a finer or more richly built bridge.

He had strong views about Londoners,

Londoners have such fierce tempers. They eat very frequently, at times more than is suitable, and are particularly fond of young swans, rabbits, deer and sea birds. They often eat mutton and beef which is generally considered to be better here than anywhere else in the world. This is due to the excellence of their pastures. The majority drink beer. For wine is very expensive, as the vine does not grown on the island.

The country

► Farming was the main activity in the country. Can you describe what each person in the picture is doing? What season of the year is it?

a Look back over the descriptions of Tudor England on page 11. How reliable are they? Would any of them fit today?

a Write out John Norden's descriptions using your own words, making it clear what he meant.

b Make a list of all the facts that the Italian visitor tells us about London and Londoners. Then make a list of those things which you think are opinions.

c Write some brief descriptions (like John Norden) of people and places that you know.

a Try to find out what the place where you live was like in Tudor times. Is there a John Norden map to help you in your local reference library?

Daily Life

Whether you had the toothache, a boil on the nose or a leg amputated, you simply had to suffer in Tudor times. Neither anaesthetics nor painkillers had been invented. People smelt more strongly than today. Only hands and faces were occasionally washed. Conversation was delivered on a wind of bad breath due to rotting teeth. Stomach troubles caused by poor food were also common. People had so many head lice that they often felt 'lousy'. Attractive, healthy people must have been a rare sight!

▶ The Shambles in York give us an idea of the narrow streets in Tudor times, with overhanging buildings on either side. Streets like this were a breeding place for rats and germs.

This is the tomb of Sir Edward Lewys, his wife and their children at Edington in Wiltshire. Few of the children survived to become adults. Deaths of children and babies were common.

Life was short. If you reached forty then you were doing well. Life was slightly better for the rich than for the poor because they did not worry all the time about where their next meal was coming from. The poor had to work very hard to survive at all.

Medicine

Doctors were of little help if you were ill. They had no training at all and treatment was nearly always bleeding. This remedy was useless against diseases like measles or diptheria. It could actually harm you.

If you broke a bone, unless it was a very simple break, the doctor would have to amputate. Doctors knew little about the importance of cleanliness.

Dress

Most people could not afford to be too fussy about the way they dressed. But for the rich, fashions in clothing changed a great deal during the Tudor period.

▶ This wedding feast took place in Bermondsey across the River Thames from the Tower of London. People are in their best clothes. Notice the differences between men and women, guests and servants.

For example, ladies' clothing was more eye-catching in the reign of Elizabeth I than before. In the reign of Henry VIII, men were the flashy dressers.

Beggars

The poor, the disabled and the unemployed were looked after by the **parish** where they were born. This was called **relief**. Everyone lived in a parish and was supposed to go to the parish church on Sundays. Churchwardens and parish constables saw that laws were obeyed and taxes collected.

▲ A nobleman and a beggar.

But as people moved about the country in search of work, this system did not work very well. A wandering beggar might be branded, have his ears bored through, be whipped or put in the stocks.

18

Schools and schooling

Education was mainly for those who could afford it. It was boys who were taught. Education was not generally provided for girls.

At least 135 free grammar schools were started in the reign of Elizabeth I. These usually charged money but kept some free places for the sons of the poor. To get in, you had to pass an entrance test when you were about seven years old.

▶ An Elizabethan schoolroom.

Discipline was strict and boys were often beaten. They learnt Latin, logic and religion. Most other subjects were not considered important enough for ordinary children to learn.

Here are some Elizabetan writing instructions.

Your thumb on your pen as highest bestow,
The forefinger next, the middle below,
And holding it thus in most comely wise,
Your body upright, stoop not with your head:
Your breast from the board if that you be wise
Lest that ye take hurt, when ye have well fed.

► English Secretary Hand. Can you work out what has been written? A new style of writing called Italian (italic) gradually became popular. Can you guess why?

a What was wrong with Tudor hygiene?

b What can we learn from the painting on pages 16-17 about Tudor life?

a Act out with some friends what happens when a wandering beggar runs into the Parish Constable.

b Carefully copy a line of English Secretary Hand.

c Imagine that you are a modern doctor or nurse taken back in time for a walk through a Tudor town. Describe those things that you see that might worry you as a doctor.

d Look at the people in the painting on pages 16-17. Choose one of the wedding guests and describe what he or she is wearing. How do these clothes compare to those worn by other people pictured in this book?

a Produce an illustrated information sheet about clothes men or women wore in Tudor times.

Tudor Houses

Tudor buildings were made from local materials because it was difficult to transport heavy goods over long distances. There were no trains, lorries or proper roads.

This Tudor farmhouse was the home of Shakespeare's mother, Mary Arden. The stone for its base and walls came from the village and the timber came from the Forest of Arden nearby. Houses were never far from a well or spring.

▶ Mary Arden's house at Wilmcote in Warwickshire.

Tudor houseowners made lists or **inventories** of their possessions. They were usually made when the owner died or made a will. These tell us the sort of furniture people had.

IN THE PARLOUR NEXT THE STREET
WHEREIN HE LODGED

Firstly, in his purse, his gown, two cloaks and his other clothes. Also, one sealed bedsted, one featherbed bolster and other bedding and curtains for that bed. Also, joined chests, one trunk and one desk and other implements.

▲ This is part of the inventory for William Marritt.

Tudor kitchens needed a large fire and fireplace because most food was cooked in a cauldron over the flames. The picture below shows how meat was roasted on spikes over the fire. This was called a spit and the person who turned it a turnspit. Tudor people began to use plates made from pottery or pewter instead of wooden plates or trenchers. Explorers brought new foods to England such as coffee, tea, potatoes, chocolate and tomatoes.

▲ The Tudor bedroom where William Shakespeare was born. Beds and bed linen were valuable possessions and were usually passed on when someone died.

▼ The kitchen at Hampton Court. What objects would you find in a modern kitchen that would not be found here ?

During early Tudor times, houses often had extensions added when they were needed in a haphazard manner. But by the time of Queen Elizabeth I, the rich had begun to build large, carefully planned houses. The country was safe enough for them to build homes without moats and fortifications.

Both these houses were built in Tudor times.

▲ Little Moreton Hall in Cheshire had parts added to it.

▶ Hardwick Hall in Derbyshire is a house that needed no extensions because it had a 'balanced design'.

◑ **a** Why do you think that the Tudors stopped fortifying their houses? Where in England might a fortified house still have been useful?

◩ **a** Make a Tudor house inventory. Imagine you live in a large farmhouse in the country. Use the pictures to help you.

b Design and make a Tudor house. Study the pictures in this book. List the building materials and where you intend to get them.

c Advertise for sale one of the houses shown in this book.

△ **a** Visit a Tudor house. Make a list of all the rooms and say what they were used for.

b Find out where the materials used to build your own house came from. Were any locally produced? Compare it with an old house nearby (Tudor, if you can find one).

The Break with Rome

The Pope, (the Bishop of Rome) was head of the christian Church. Not everyone was happy with the way the Church was run. They thought that it did not follow Jesus Christ's teaching closely enough and so they protested. These Protestants tried to change or reform the Church. We call this the **Reformation** and it started in Germany in 1517.

▶ Henry's title 'Defender of the Faith', (Fid. Def. or FD) is still used by British monarchs. Can you see where?

▼ Miles Coverdale's translation was the first complete Bible in English (1536).

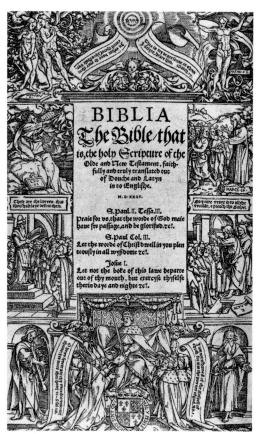

The Pope gave Henry VIII the title Defender of the Faith. But, some years later, Henry VIII had a row with the Pope. The Pope did not allow Henry to divorce his first wife, Catherine of Aragon. Henry wanted to marry Anne Boleyn and have a son and heir. Henry declared that he was the head of the Church in England, not the Pope. Laws were passed taking away the Pope's powers in England (Act of Supremacy, 1534) and Henry married Anne Boleyn.

When the Church in England became separate from Rome, it also began to change or reform. Bibles in English were illegal up until the break with Rome. Bible stories were told, not read, because they were written in Latin which ordinary people could not read.

Bible stories were painted as pictures on church walls or shown in the stained glass of church windows. Henry VIII changed all this. He ordered that Bibles in English should be placed in every church. Most of the old catholic ways of worshipping were seen as superstitious. Sculptures and shrines, jewels and tapestries, and paintings on church walls were done away with.

▶ A wall painting on a church in Hertfordshire.

Monasteries

Henry VIII decided to get rid of the wealthy **monasteries** and make himself rich at the same time. The monks were obedient to the Pope, not the king. Many people thought monks were rich and lazy so few tried to stop him. A special law was passed in 1536 and within three years 560 monasteries were closed. This is called the **dissolution of the monasteries**. Fine buildings were destroyed, jewellery sold and church plate melted down for cash. Monks and nuns were made homeless.

▶ This drawing shows monks at prayer. Monks spent their time praying, farming their huge areas of land, looking after travellers by giving them food and a bed and copying out books.

▼ Some very grand monasteries, like Fountains Abbey in Yorkshire, were destroyed.

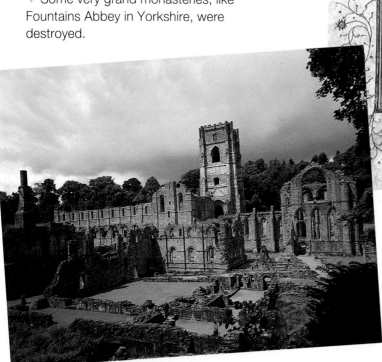

The Church went on changing after Henry VIII died and England became a protestant country.

Traditions like maypoles and Plough Monday gatherings were stopped. The 'Mass' was renamed 'Holy Communion'. To make sure that everyone worshipped in the same way a book of Common Prayer was produced. A similar book is still used in the Church of England.

Ordinary people were often confused. Many stopped going to church altogether. Some found the new 'Prayer Book' services so boring that they laughed and talked all the way through them. In Coventry, 'bouncers' had to keep order in church. Catholics in the north of England were so upset by the changes that they rebelled. The rebellions were all put down.

◗ **a** What made a Catholic different from a Protestant? Do Catholics and Protestants disagree so violently today?

◩ **a** Design a wall painting to tell people who cannot read one of the stories in the Bible.

b Look carefully at the photograph of Fountains Abbey on page 26 and make a sketch, based on the photograph, of what it might have looked like before it was destroyed. What other evidence will help you do this?

⚠ **a** Examine the language in a Book of Common Prayer. List the main differences from today's speech.

b Find out more about monasteries. Do you think that Henry VIII was right to close them down? Were all monks rich and lazy?

War

England and France often fought each other to decide who should rule parts of France. However, in 1520, England and France made peace. Henry VIII invited Francis I, King of France, to a banquet and tournament in Northern France.

At the time, it was said to be the eighth wonder of the world. No money was spared, fountains even spouted wine. Because the English tents were made of crimson and gold cloth, it is known as the Field of Cloth of Gold.

This painting was made of the event showing everything happening at once. Henry VIII is riding to

▶ A painting of the Field of Cloth of Gold.

the meeting (left centre) but at the same time is meeting Francis I on foot (centre top) in front of a tent of cloth of gold. A jousting tournament is in progress (top right), the guns of Guisnes Castle (on the left) are firing a salute and a feast is being eaten (right). Overhead, a dragon represents a dramatic firework rocket used in one of the displays. Henry VIII and his wife, Catherine of Aragon, stayed at the palace (centre right). It was specially built by 6000 workmen and was a painted tent. It was hoped that this event was the beginning of a friendship between France and England. But, after two years of peace, they were at war again.

The *Mary Rose*

Twenty-five years later, when England was again at war with France, Henry VIII captured Boulogne. Francis I sent a fleet of ships to attack England. It was larger than the Spanish Armada (see pages 32 - 35) with 235 ships and 30 000 men and it sailed round the Isle of Wight to attack Portsmouth. Henry VIII watched the battle from Southsea castle.

Eventually, on Sunday 19th July 1545, when the wind changed direction, the English fleet of 60 ships led by the ships *Great Harry* and the *Mary Rose*, sailed out to meet the French. Disaster struck. Water entered through the gunports of the *Mary Rose*. She sank so fast that most of her crew drowned. Nobody knows why she sank. The French thought they had sunk her but it might have been because she was overloaded. The sailors on board were not well-disciplined. The captain of the *Mary Rose* shouted during the battle that he had 'the sort of knaves he could not rule'. Of the 700 men on board, about a dozen were saved. But the French invasion failed, for after attacking the Isle of Wight, the French went home.

▼ Henry VIII leaving Dover for the Field of Cloth of Gold in 1520. One of the ships on the left is probably the *Mary Rose* named after Mary, the king's favourite sister.

An Admiral of the French fleet wrote,

The galleys advanced on the British whilst at anchor to provoke them into engagement. The weather favoured our attempt for it was calm. Our galleys had all the advantages of working. The English for want of a wind not being able to stir. Hardly a shot missed them. Among other damages the English received, the *Mary Rose*, one of their principal ships, was sunk by cannon.

When the *Mary Rose* was raised from the sea in 1982, many objects were recovered.

► A bronze gun.

▲ Navigational instruments. A slate protractor, a pocket sundial and a pair of brass dividers.

▼ Personal items which might have been owned by the ships officers. There is a comb, a rosary and a die among the items.

◐ **a** Why was there so much trouble between England and France in Tudor times?

◩ **a** Choose to be one of the people shown in the picture 'Field of Cloth of Gold'. Write a report on the day's events from your point of view.

b Draw, paint or make a picture or model of a Tudor warship, being accurate with the detail.

c Why did the *Mary Rose* sink? Investigate the sinking and report on your findings, based on the evidence.

△ **a** Find out about the raising of the *Mary Rose*. What evidence has been discovered by this project?

The Spanish Armada

During the reign of Elizabeth I, England and Spain became enemies. English ships attacked Spanish ships wherever they found them. England also helped Dutch rebels to fight against a Spanish army in the Spanish Netherlands. King Philip II of Spain became fed up with the meddling English and wanted to help Catholics in England. Spain was a catholic country and England was protestant so Elizabeth was Philip's chief enemy. An invasion fleet was planned by Philip. This Armada would sail up the English Channel, pick-up an army from the Netherlands and land on the south coast of England.

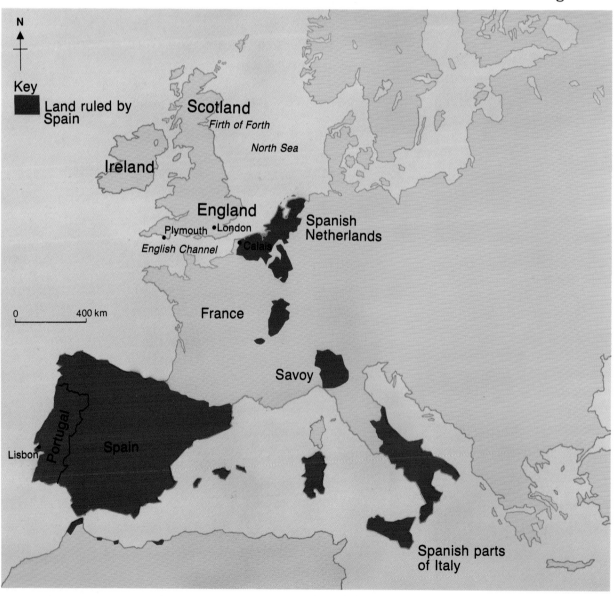

N

Key

◼ Land ruled by Spain

Scotland

Firth of Forth

North Sea

Ireland

England

Plymouth ● London

English Channel ● Calais

Spanish Netherlands

0   400 km

France

Savoy

Lisbon

Portugal

Spain

Spanish parts of Italy

Invasion diary

May 1588: 130 ships of the Armada leave Lisbon, in Portugal, with 30 000 men.

July 1588: 124 ships reach the English Channel.

The Duke of Medina-Sidonia, leader of the Armada, wrote in his diary,

At dawn, the Armada was very near the shore. We were seen by the people on land, who made signal fires. We then discovered that the English fleet had left Plymouth.

20th July: Admiral Howard sails from Plymouth with nearly 60 ships of the English fleet. He attacks the Armada from the west.

24th July: Skirmishes continue. 40 more ships join the English fleet which is then organised into four squadrons led by Drake, Frobisher, Hawkins and Howard.

27th July: The Armada anchors off Calais.

28th July (night): Attacks by English fireships cause the Armada to cut anchors to escape.

▶ This painting shows the English fire ships attacking the Spanish Armada.

Medina-Sidonia's diary gives his view of the battle,

The English fleet, with the wind and tide in its favour, was catching up with us very quickly. In order to save my ships, I decided to face the whole of the enemy's fleet. The enemy's flagship attacked our flagship with great fury at daybreak, coming within musket-shot. The attack lasted until three in the afternoon and the artillery fire did not stop for one moment. My ship was so much damaged with cannon-shot that the leaks could not be stopped and her rigging was almost cut to shreds.

29th July: The Armada is swept north by winds and cannot get back into port. The English attack, sinking 7 ships.

30th July: Strong gales drive the Armada into the North Sea. Howard follows as far as the Firth of Forth.

The Armada struggles homeward around Scotland and Ireland because the wind made it impossible to return to the English Channel. Many ships are lost on the way.

▶ A Tudor map showing the route that the Spanish Armada took.

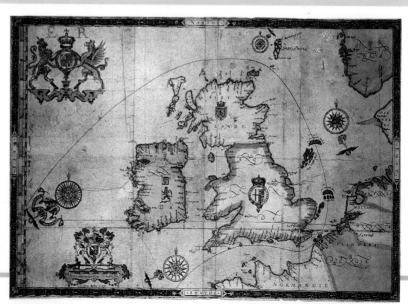

In recent years a number of Spanish wrecks have been explored and objects discovered.

► These cannons were found off the coast of Northern Ireland.

▼ Coins found on the Spanish ship, the *Girona*. They were a month's wages for a Spanish sailor.

◐ **a** Most of the Armada was destroyed by the natural forces of sea and weather. Should England claim victory?

◧ **a** Imagine that it was possible to produce daily news flashes at the time of the Armada. Write Armada 'news flashes' for broadcasting on radio or television.

b Draw an illustrated map of the Armada's voyage from its start to its finish.

△ **a** Find out more about what happened after the Armada had returned home. Did England and Spain make peace?

Explorers, Traders and Settlers

It takes a great deal of courage to sail out into the open sea when you have no idea what might happen to you. In spite of the dangers, many voyages of exploration were made in Tudor times. Curiosity was one reason but men also searched for riches such as gold, silver and ivory. Some wanted new lands in which to live, others hoped to reach the rich countries of the East by sea where spices, silks and gems could be traded.

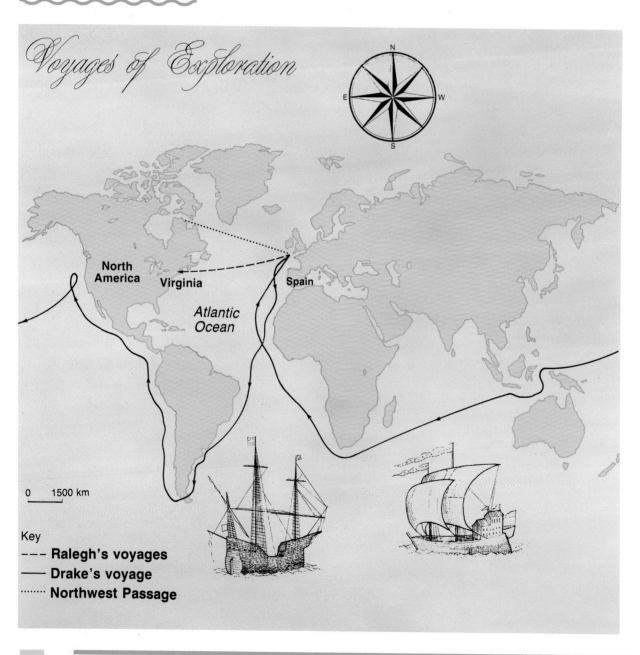

Voyages of Exploration

North America

Virginia

Spain

Atlantic Ocean

0   1500 km

Key
- - - **Ralegh's voyages**
—— **Drake's voyage**
······· **Northwest Passage**

▶ This picture of John Cabot, the explorer, was painted 100 years ago. It shows Cabot (dressed in black) boarding his ship in Bristol in 1497. He sailed across the Atlantic Ocean hoping to find a new way to the East. Instead he found North America and was the first European to sail up the coast of Newfoundland.

When the Tudors started to explore the world, they often found that the Spanish and Portuguese had got there first. England was soon fighting these countries. The English attacked the Spanish in America and on their treasure ships as they crossed the Atlantic Ocean.

Francis Drake was the first Englishman to travel around the world (from 1577 to 1580). Other English sailors like John Hawkins, Martin Frobisher and Henry Hudson tried to find a new way to reach the East by sailing north-westwards but were stopped by ice. Sir Walter Ralegh made a journey to North America in 1585.

▶ The English arriving in North America. Why are there people in rowing boats in this picture? What are the people doing on land?

Ralegh tells us about an encounter on one of his voyages,

The king of the Aromaia came and with him many women and children to wonder at our nation. They brought us venison, pork, hens, chickens, fowl, fish, with divers sorts of excellent fruits, and roots and a great abundance of Pinas, the princess of fruits that grow under the sun. One of them gave me a beast, called by the Spaniards Armadilla, which seemed to be barred over with small plates like a Renocero [Rhinocerus]. After the old king had rested I began to talk with him by my interpreter. I marvelled to find him a man of such gravity and judgement yet he had no help of learning.

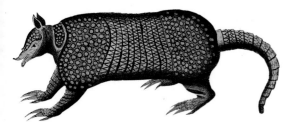

▼ An armadillo.

▶ These are some of the foods Ralegh ate on his voyages. Fresh food did not last long on long sea voyages so the fruit and meat brought to him by the king of Aromaia must have been very welcome.

◖ **a** Why did the Europeans want to explore the world?

◩ **a** Study the routes taken by Tudor explorers on a map or globe. Can you find any names of places, named after famous people or events?

b Imagine you are a Tudor explorer. Write a diary of one of your voyages and plot your voyage on an outline map of the world.

△ **a** List the animals and foods that were new to the explorers of America.

The life of Ralegh (1552-1618)

Walter Ralegh was born at Hayes near the seaside village of Budleigh Salterton in Devon. When he was a small boy he probably heard sailors telling stories of their adventures at sea.

▲ John Millais painted this picture of Ralegh (left) on the beach at Budleigh Salterton in 1870. Millais never met Ralegh. (How can we be certain?) How accurate do you think the picture is?

Ralegh enjoyed reading books and was sent to be educated at Oxford University. At the age of 17, he chose to do something more adventurous and went off to fight in a Protestant army in France.

Ralegh's first voyage

Ralegh's first voyage as an explorer began in 1578. With six other ships, he sailed from Devon as captain of a heavily-armed vessel of 100 tonnes called the *Falcon*. Actually he was more like a pirate than an explorer. He hoped to capture Spanish galleons that were taking gold and jewels from South America to Spain but he found none. Ralegh's ships turned back when they reached the Azores.

Ralegh then decided to seek his fortune in London. Instead of finding riches, he found prison. He spent six days in the Fleet prison for fighting, and further time in the Marshalsea prison for causing "a fray beside the tennis court at Westminster".

▶ Tennis was very popular amongst the wealthy in Tudor times.

◀ Tudor tennis balls were made of leather and stuffed with hair. Compare the tennis ball in the photograph with the modern one.

Rich and famous

Next Ralegh found employment as a captain in the army and had a bit of luck. Important letters had to be taken from Ireland to Queen Elizabeth in London. Ralegh got the job.

One story tells how Ralegh saw Queen Elizabeth about to step out of her coach into a pool of water. Quickly he rushed forward and laid his coat over the puddle. Whether this happened or not, the handsome Ralegh was certainly noticed by the Queen and soon became one of her favourites.

Queen Elizabeth gave Ralegh important work to do, as well as gifts of land and money. He was made captain of the Queen's guard, Vice-Admiral of the Western Counties and given the title *Sir* Walter Ralegh.

▶ Ralegh and his son Walter. Ralegh was a big, good-looking young man, six feet tall with thick black hair. He spent as much money as he could afford on clothes so he always looked smart.

Life at court

Many young men like Walter Ralegh, dressed-up in their finest clothes and hung around the **Court** trying to attract the Queen's attention. It was one way of getting a job.

The Court was the place where the Queen, her ministers and her secretaries and servants lived. Important people at Court were called **courtiers.**

Much business was discussed at Court, it was mostly to do with wars and money. After supper came music and dancing. The *volta* was a very energetic dance. Gentlemen had to remove their swords before dancing it to avoid hurting themselves.

▶ This is probably Queen Elizabeth doing the *volta* at Court. Dancers had to leap up and spin round in the *volta*.

During the summer, Elizabeth usually took her Court on a **progress** around the country. Hundreds of carts loaded with servants and courtiers, clothes and furniture, moved from one large country house to another. To entertain the Queen was expensive. When she stayed for three days with Lord North, the Court consumed 1,200 chickens, 2,500 eggs, 67 sheep, 34 pigs and 33 geese.

Ralegh's last adventure

Ralegh spent a great deal of his own money trying to build a **colony** in Virginia (North America) but with little success. One settlement of 108 men, women and children had vanished without trace when people went back to visit them several years later. Plants, including tobacco and the potato, were brought back from Virginia. Potatoes were planted at Ralegh's home in Ireland.

Ralegh had many adventurous voyages. He searched for gold in South America; captured Spanish treasure ships, and was wounded fighting the Spanish at Cadiz. Even getting married was a daring adventure for Ralegh. The Queen threw him into prison when she found out that his girlfriend was one of her maids, Elizabeth Throgmorton. The Queen had not given her permission! Ralegh married Throgmorton but was banned from attending Court.

When Queen Elizabeth died, Ralegh's enemies plotted against him. He was accused of being a **traitor** and imprisoned in the Bloody Tower. During the many years he spent in the Tower of London, he carried out scientific experiments, made medicines and wrote a history of the world.

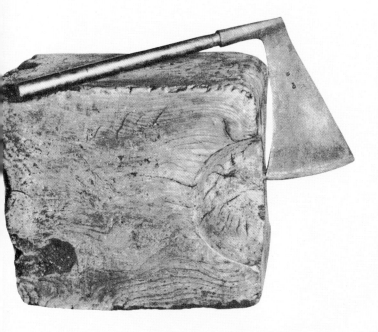

Finally, Ralegh was released and went once more to South America in search of gold. Unfortunately he found none and his son was killed fighting the Spanish. Back in England, the Spanish ambassador demanded that Ralegh should be executed. With few friends left at Court to help him, Ralegh was doomed. In 1618 he was beheaded.

◄ Important people were executed by having their heads chopped off.

Musicians and Writers

Music-making was something that most people enjoyed. Every educated person was expected to be able to read music and to sing a part in a song or **madrigal.** Rich children learned to play the lute which was the most popular instrument. The most famous English composers during Tudor times were John Taverner, Thomas Tallis, William Byrd and Orlando Gibbons. Even Henry VIII composed music.

▲ A group of musicians. What instruments can you see?

A rich music-lover, Sir Thomas Kitson, listed his collection of musical instruments in his **inventory** of 1603,

... four lutes, two luting books made of leather, six viols, six violins, a case of seven recorders, four cornets, a bandora, a cittern, two sackbuts, three hautboys, two flutes and a great pair of double virginals.

▶ Queen Elizabeth playing the lute. Many musical instruments were improved during the Tudor period and cellos and violins were made for the first time. In her old age, Elizabeth saw the recorder replace the lute as the most fashionable instrument. The fashion started in Italy where lots of new ideas in music came from.

Plays and players

Queen Elizabeth enjoyed watching plays so play-writing was encouraged. The plots were usually very bloodthirsty and violent, but life could be like that in Tudor times.

In 1577 the actor-manager, James Burbage, erected a building called 'The Theatre' just for performing plays. It was the first of its kind. Before that, actors performed in the courtyards of inns. Women did not act in plays. Young boys played all the female parts.

▲ The Globe theatre, on the south bank of the River Thames, where many of Shakespeare's plays were performed. It was circular and had a thatched roof. It burnt down in 1613.

▶ The Globe Theatre is being rebuilt. It will look, as near as possible, how it did in Tudor times.

Shakespeare

Many new books were printed in Tudor times although you needed a licence to do so. Some people believe that the English language was at its most beautiful in Tudor times and that William Shakespeare's plays and poetry contain some of the greatest writing in English. Shakespeare was born in 1564 and died in 1616.

▲ William Shakespeare.

Winter

When icicles hang by the wall,
And Dick the shepherd blows his nail.
And Tom bears logs into the hall,
And milk comes frozen home in the pail;
When blood is nipped, and ways be foul
Then nightly sings the staring owl
                    Tu-who;

Tu-whit, tu-who - a merry note,
While greasy Joan doth keel the pot.

When all aloud the wind doth blow,
And coughing drowns the parson's saw,
And birds sit brooding in the snow,
And Marian's nose looks red and raw,
When roasted crabs hiss in the bowl,
Then nightly sings the staring owl
                    Tu-who;

Tu-whit, tu-who - a merry note,
While greasy Joan doth keel the pot.

William Shakespeare's poem gives us a picture of what winter was like before the invention of central heating. Greasy Joan does not make the kitchen sound very hygienic!

a Paint Shakespeare's picture of winter. Learn the poem and recite it out loud.

b List the music-making equipment that you have in your home. How does it compare with Sir Thomas Kitson's list?

Glossary

ambassador An important official from another country who lived in England and represented his government here.

biography The story of someone's life.

colony A group of people who settle in a foreign country.

Court The place where the queen, her ministers, secretaries and servants lived.

courtiers Important people who lived at Court.

dissolution of the monasteries The deliberate breaking-up of monasteries and the seizing of their money and goods by Henry VIII.

dynasty A family of rulers that reign for more than one generation.

Gaelic The languages of the Celtic people.

inventory A list of belongings.

madrigal A type of song, popular in Tudor times.

monarch A king or a queen.

monastery A place, centred on a church, where a community of men spent most of their time in religious activities.

parish A local area, centred on a church and village, in which the taxes were collected and the poor looked after.

portrait A drawing or painting of someone.

progress A journey the Queen and her household often took around England in the summer.

Protestant A branch of the Christian church which separated from the Catholic church during the reign of Henry VIII.

Reformation The changes made to the Catholic Church which led to the setting up of Protestant churches.

relief Charity given to needy people within a parish.

traitor A person who betrays their own country.

Tudor The ruling dynasty of England from 1485 to 1603.

Index

Act of Supremacy 24
Act of Union 8
America, North 37, 43
America, South 40, 43
Anne of Cleves 5
Armada, Spanish 3, 32-35

beggars 18
Bible, the 2, 24, 25
Boleyn, Anne 5, 24
books 46

Cabot, John 37
Catherine of Aragon 5, 24, 29
Catholics 3, 24, 25, 27, 32
Church of England 24-25, 27
colonies 43
Cornwall 8
countryside 13, 23
court life 42

dancing 42
dissolution of the monasteries 26
doctors 15
Drake, Sir Francis 37
dress 16-17

Edward VI 3, 5
Elizabeth I 5, 6-7, 8, 10, 32, 41, 42
explorers 22, 36-38
  Walter Ralegh 39-44
Field of the Cloth of Gold 28-29
Flodden, Battle of 8
food 12, 22, 38, 42, 43
France 8, 28, 30
  war with 28-31
Francis I, King of France 28, 29, 30
Frobisher, Sir Martin 37
furniture 21-22

gold 36, 40, 43

Hampton Court 2, 22
Hawkins, Sir John 37
health 14-15
Henry VII 4
Henry VIII 4, 5, 9, 24, 25, 26, 28, 29, 30
  wives 5
houses 21-23
  kitchens 22
Howard, Catherine 5
Hudson, Henry 37

Ireland 8, 9

Latin 19, 24
London 11-12
  buildings 12

mapmaking 10
Mary I 3, 6
Mary Rose, the 30-31
monasteries 26
music 44
  composers 44
  instruments 44

Netherlands 32
Norden, John 10-11

paintings 4
Parr, Catherine 5
Philip II, King of Spain 32
plants, new 43
Pope, the 24
Protestants 3, 24, 27

Ralegh, Sir Walter 37, 38, 39-43
Reformation 24
religion and churches 24-27
Richard III 4

schools 19-20
Scotland 8
Seymour, Jane 5
Shakespeare 21, 46-47
ships 30-31
Spain 3
  war with 32-35
spices 36

tennis 40
theatres 45
  Globe 45
tournaments 9
trade 36

Wales 8
war
  with France 28-31
  with Spain 32-35

Acknowledgements

The publishers would like to thank the following for permission to reproduce photographic material:
(t = top, b = bottom, r = right) A.F. Kersting pp14, 26 (b). Barnaby's Picture Library pp2 (b), 43(b). Bodelian Library p20. The Bridgeman Art Library p4, 39, 42, 44(b) and cover. British Library pp10, 13, 26 (r). Ollie Hatch p38. Clive Hicks ARPS pp15, 25. College of Arms p9. e.t. archive pp12, 19, 37, 45. Mary Evans Picture Library p37(b). Fotomas Index pp11 (both), 18, by permission of the Marquess of Salisbury p16-17. The Mansell Collection pp40(t), 43(t). Mary Rose Trust p31 (both). The Museum of London p40(b). National Maritime Museum pp3 (b) and cover, 33, 34. National Portrait Gallery pp3 (tx2), p5(b), 7, 41, 44 (t). National Trust Photographic Library p22 (b). National Trust/Mike Williams p23 (both). The Royal Collection, HM the Queen pp6, 28-29, 30. Royal Mint p24. Shakespeare Birthplace Trust p46. Ulster Museum p35 (both). Chris Wright pp21, 22 (t).